FOR

# THE CHALLENGER SALE

## Taking Control of the Customer Conversation

# Krystal Reads

# This workbook belong to

# Copyright © by Krystal Reads 2024

## All Rights Reserved

# How To Use This Workbook

Welcome to the companion Workbook for the book "The Challenger Sale" by Matthew Dixon and Brent Adamson,

This Workbook was carefully designed by Krystal Reads with an aim to act as your road map for revolutionary success, your business acumen and sales skills.

Using this game-changing resource to its full potential is as follows:

Commence with the Goal:

Make a clear list of your objectives for company expansion and sales. Utilizing the knowledge from "The Challenger Sale," determine your goals.

Overviews of each Chapter:

Dip into the illuminating chapter summaries to get started. Before diving in further, quickly review the main ideas and areas of interest.

Important Lesson Integration:

Explore the salient points that are offered. Envision each lesson's applicability in your company setting and consider how it aligns with your present sales approach.

Action Plans:

Treat action plans with zeal. For organized implementation, they are your dynamic tools.

See quantifiable outcomes by tailoring the tactics to your company's requirements.

Novel Ways to Encourage Participation:

Utilize the creative inspirations offered to actively participate. These are meant to help you get a deeper knowledge and to spark critical thinking. They range from the Performance Audit to the Challenger Mindset Assessment.

Doable Tasks for Practical Use in the Real World

Engage in hands-on activities that bring theory to life. Turn information into results by actively incorporating the book's contents into your approach, mentality, and sales methods.
Reflection that is Regular:

Always evaluate your own development. Assist yourself and your sales strategy with continuous self-evaluation by using the workbook.
Increase Your Learning Potential .

Go back over chapters, review and make adjustments to your action plans if necessary. This dynamic workbook is designed to change as you do.

Take advantage of this workbook as your unique manual for understanding "The Challenger Sale." On your way to sales excellence and company success, may your life-changing experience be enlightening, fulfilling, and influential.

# Introduction

"The Challenger Sale" provides a better way to deal with customers and is also a great tool for managing coaching, training salespeople, and building client loyalty.

The book, written by managing directors Matthew Dixon and Brent Adamson of CEB's Sales Executive Council in Washington, D.C., is based on a comprehensive research that CEB Inc. performed with thousands of sales professionals from a variety of businesses. Dixon and Adamson contend that managing complicated and significant B2B solutions requires a different strategy than the conventional one of fostering connections.

Fundamentally, the book presents a novel way to sales called the "Challenger" strategy, which outperforms traditional methods of fostering relationships. Salespeople take charge of the sales process by pushing consumers to think about new ideas in line with the "Challenger" sales strategy. In addition, challengers are distinguished by their readiness to resist rather than just comply with client requests. The writers explore the particular abilities and dispositions that support the achievement of people who embrace a challenger attitude.

**Date:**

**Goals**

# CHAPTER 1

## GETTING AROUND THE SOLUTION SELLING LANDSCAPE

The transition from conventional single-product sales to the dynamic domain of solution selling represents a significant change in the corporate environment. This change is characterized by a shift away from simple product offerings and toward packaged solutions with a foundation in strategic consulting. This shift is being driven by suppliers' proactive efforts to prevent commoditization and create obstacles that make it difficult for rivals to imitate their value offerings. But this change brings with it a new set of difficulties for suppliers and clients alike.

Consumers increasingly want a more cooperative decision-making process as they search for practical answers. It becomes critical for the varied team members to get an agreement and to want to transfer the risk to the suppliers. Additionally, clients are seeking more specialized solutions and consulting services to help them through the complexities of intricate transactions. In the context of this evolving market, providers participating in solution selling must prioritize flexibility and strategic thinking.

In this exciting new realm of solution selling, there are a few important things for suppliers to keep in mind. First of all, in this situation, high achievers become very desirable. The performance gap of 59% exists between ordinary and star performers in a transactional selling environment.

If, therefore, the core, or average performers, are not developed, there is a significant danger. If left unchecked, they can fall behind to the point that they can't carry out solution sales in an efficient manner. Therefore, it is essential for suppliers to develop the skills of the larger sales force in addition to identifying and fostering top performers.

As the story progresses, the chapter presents five different sales personas, each of which captures a particular quality shared by real-world sales personnel. The Hard Worker, The Relationship Builder, The Lone Wolf, The Reactive Problem Solver, and The Challenger are the characters that serve as the foundation for comprehending the various strategies used by sales representatives in solution selling. In-depth discussions of these personalities and their consequences for difficult sales are provided in the following sections.

The study results from CEB provide important light on how these personalities are distributed across core and star performers. Among the top achievers, the Challenger character stands out as a crucial factor, accounting for about 40% of this select group. Within the complex solution selling environment, where mastery of complex sales techniques is critical, challengers—who make up over half of the top performers in the complicated sales arena —become vital agents of success for a sales team. This chapter provides a framework for a thorough examination of these personalities and a road map for negotiating the many possibilities and problems found in the exciting new field of solution selling.

# Key Lessons

## Lesson 1 : **Solution Selling**

Embrace the shift from conventional single-product sales to solution selling, which entails putting together packaged products with a strategic consulting foundation.

## Lesson 2 : **Suppliers' Strategic Positioning**

Recognize the tactics suppliers use to stay out of the commoditization market and to put up obstacles for rivals looking to copy their products.

## Lesson 3 : **Collaborative Decision-Making**

As clients look for collaborative decision-making procedures, acknowledge that a growing agreement among varied team members is required.

## Lesson 4 : **Value of Top Performers**

Recognize that in solution selling, when the difference in performance between average and star performers becomes much larger, top performers have a higher value.

## Lesson 5 : **Core Performer Development**

Recognize how crucial it is to close the performance gap between top and core performers in order to maintain the sales team's overall efficacy.

**Action Plan 1**

### Skill Development Blueprint

**NOTE**

Create a customized strategy to improve your solution selling abilities, emphasizing areas found by asking yourself self-reflection questions.

**Action Plan 1**

### Challenger Integration Strategy

**NOTE**

Describe how you will incorporate Challenger techniques into your sales process step-by-step. Set benchmarks and quantifiable objectives to help you embrace the Challenger attitude.

**Action Plan 1**

### Team Performance Enhancement Initiative

**NOTE**

Work together with your teammates to create a plan that will help close the performance difference between average and exceptional performers. To increase the overall efficacy of the team in solution selling, set common goals and take concrete actionable initiatives.

| Goals | Action Plan |
| --- | --- |
|  |  |
|  |  |
|  |  |
|  |  |
|  |  |
|  |  |
|  |  |
|  |  |
|  |  |
|  |  |
|  |  |

## Final Results

Do you still adhere to conventional transactional methods, or are you now embracing solution selling?

_____

_____

_____

_____

_____

_____

_____

How well-versed in the tactics suppliers use to stave off commoditization are you? How can you implement such tactics in your work

_____

_____

_____

_____

_____

_____

_____

In your encounters with customers, are you encouraging cooperative decision-making among various team members?

_____

_____

_____

_____

_____

_____

How successfully can you
address the desire for more
personalization in your products
while navigating the risk moving
onto suppliers?

_____

_____

_____

_____

_____

_____

_____

In your sales environment, are
you aware of the difference in
performance between average
and top performers, and if so,
where do you now stand?

_____

_____

_____

_____

_____

_____

How can you help your sales staff
close the performance difference
between core and top
performers?

_____

_____

_____

_____

_____

_____

Which sales persona—The Hard Worker, The Relationship Builder, The Lone Wolf, The Reactive Problem Solver, or The Challenger—do you most identify with?

_____

_____

_____

_____

_____

_____

Are you aware of how often Challengers are among top performers? If so, how can you use Challenger tactics in your strategy?

_____

_____

_____

_____

_____

_____

To what extent are you dedicated to honing your skills, particularly in relation to solution selling and the Challenger mindset?

_____

_____

_____

_____

_____

_____

# EXERCISES

## Sales Persona Reflection :

**1**

*WHAT DO YOU THINK?*

Examine your sales personas and the ways in which your present strategy reflects the traits of each persona. Determine which areas need to be improved or adjusted.

_____

_____

_____

## Challenger Integration Strategy :

**2**

*WHAT DO YOU THINK?*

Describe how you will incorporate Challenger techniques into your sales process step-by-step. Set benchmarks and quantifiable objectives to help you embrace the Challenger attitude.

_____

_____

_____

## Team Performance Enhancement Initiative :

**3**

*WHAT DO YOU THINK?*

Work together with your teammates to create a plan that will help close the performance difference between average and exceptional performers. To increase the overall efficacy of the team in solution selling, set common goals and take concrete actionable initiatives..

_____

_____

_____

_____

In light of solution selling and the many sales personas, have you determined any areas in which you need to improve both personally and professionally?

_____

_____

_____

_____

_____

_____

In your sales initiatives, how effectively do you strike a balance between self-motivation and process-oriented efforts?

_____

_____

_____

_____

_____

_____

Are you committed to giving clients excellent service and fostering long-lasting relationships?

_____

_____

_____

_____

_____

_____

How much do you follow organizational procedures vs following your instincts, and how does it affect achieving your goals?

_____

_____

_____

_____

_____

_____

What areas do you push executives in your business to think differently about challenging situations by providing fresh perspectives?

_____

_____

_____

_____

Have you looked at techniques to improve your skills and help your sales team execute challenging deals successfully?

_____

_____

_____

_____

# FINAL RESULTS TRACKER

## THE MOST IMPORTANT GOAL I ACHIEVED

## HOW DID I ACHIEVE IT?

## PERSONAL NOTE :

## HOW CAN I KEEP IT UP

## THINGS I'M GRATEFUL FOR:

## LESSONS LEARNED

# CHAPTER 2

## UNCOVERING THE CHALLENGER APPROACH'S POWER

The second chapter in the complex world of B2B sales opens with a startling realization: the sales process itself is the key to retaining customers, not a product, service, price, or brand. Remarkably, 53 percent of customer loyalty can be traced back to a sales representative's interactions with their customers. This finding has a significant influence on the conversation about successful sales tactics.

This chapter presents a taxonomy of business-to-business sales reps, grouping them into five categories according to their abilities and customer-facing behaviors:

- 1. THE HARD WORKER: A resilient and self-driven sales professional who appreciates criticism and growth.
- 2. THE LONE WOLF: A confident person who follows their gut and produces outcomes but poses management difficulties.
- 3. THE RELATIONSHIP BUILDER: An excellent consultative representative who thrives at establishing rapport with potential clients.
- 4. THE CHALLENGER: A salesperson who has a distinct point of view, enjoys a good argument, and is very knowledgeable about the client's Industry.
- 5. THE PROBLEM SOLVER: A trustworthy, detail-oriented representative committed to finding solutions for any issue that comes up.

The core of 'The Challenger Sale' is the examination of the 'Challenger Approach,' a set of techniques closely associated with the sales output of high achievers. Based on a thorough examination of sales professionals, the research reveals an intriguing finding: 40% of top performers in sales choose the Challenger style, setting it apart from the other four selling approaches.

Additionally, the chapter clarifies that strong achievers are twice as likely to choose the Challenger strategy over other techniques. More than half of top performers choose the Challenger profile when it comes to difficult sales, where the hurdles are greater. Remarkably, just 7% of high achievers choose the relationship-building strategy, highlighting the unique potency of the Challenger technique.

The Challenger strategy has a more nuanced success trajectory; as sales complexity increases, so does its effectiveness, which is especially felt by top performers. The strategy works just as well for typical users as it does for users of other approaches. This discovery highlights the Challenger Approach as a powerful tactic for those hoping to reach the pinnacles of high sales performance and provokes critical thought about how well one's sales approach aligns with market expectations. As the chapter progresses, it encourages readers to delve further into the subtleties of the Challenger technique, presenting it as a guide for attaining greatness in the ever-changing world of business-to-business sales.

# Key Lessons

## Lesson 1 : <u>Sales Experience as the Driver</u>

Recognize that sales experience has a greater impact on customer loyalty than other considerations such as brand, price, service, or product.

## Lesson 2 : <u>Characteristics of B2B Sales Representatives</u>

The Hard Worker, The Lone Wolf, The Relationship Builder, The Challenger, and The Problem Solver are the five different characteristics of B2B sales representatives that you should get familiar with. Each profile describes certain talents and habits in client interactions.

## Lesson 3 : <u>Challenger Approach Dominance</u>

Admit that the Challenger Approach is the most popular selling approach, since 40 percent of top sales performers use it, outperforming other approaches.

## Lesson 4 : <u>Double Likelihood for top Performers</u>

Highlight the Challenger approach's efficacy in boosting sales success by recognizing that top performers are twice as likely to employ it as other methods.

## Lesson 5 : <u>Challenger's Success in complicated Sales</u>

It is noteworthy that over 50% of top performers favor the Challenger profile in complicated sales, demonstrating its adeptness in handling difficult commercial exchanges.

### Quantifiable Objectives

Creating a detailed strategy to include Challenger methods into your sales approach is necessary. To monitor your development, pinpoint particular areas that need work and establish quantifiable objectives.

**NOTE**

---

**Action Plan 1**

### Skill Development plan

Make a customized plan to improve the skills related to the Challenger methodology. Set a deadline for skill improvement and prioritize the areas that need work.

**NOTE**

---

**Action Plan 1**

### Enhancement of Team Dynamics Project

Put out a plan for your sales team to investigate and comprehend each member's sales persona as a group. Determine how to improve the overall performance of the team in B2B sales by using the strengths of several personas.

**NOTE**

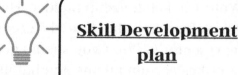

| Goals | Action Plan |
|---|---|
|  |  |
|  |  |
|  |  |
|  |  |
|  |  |
|  |  |
|  |  |
|  |  |
|  |  |

## Final Results

Have you thought about how your sales interactions affect your customers' loyalty, and have you identified the sales experience as a major motivator?

_____

_____

_____

_____

_____

_____

Are you aware that top sales performers tend to use the Challenger Approach more often than not? If so, how does this knowledge influence your own approach?

_____

_____

_____

_____

_____

Which selling style do you feel is more in line with—the Challenger method or another?

_____

_____

_____

_____

_____

_____

Are you aware of the possibility that strong performers would choose the Challenger strategy over others, given your performance goals?

_____

_____

_____

_____

_____

_____

_____

Do you already use a process similar to the Challenger approach in complicated sales circumstances, or do you look into other options?

_____

_____

_____

_____

_____

How can you strike a compromise between the need of fostering relationships and the knowledge that only 7% of high achievers choose this course of action?

_____

_____

_____

_____

_____

Are you aware of the Challenger approach's varied success trajectory, especially how well it works in difficult sales situations?

_____

_____

_____

_____

_____

_____

Given that 40% of top performers adopt a Challenger style, have you given your sales strategy a critical evaluation?

_____

_____

_____

_____

_____

_____

Which approach—the self-driven, tenacious Hard Worker—better describes you, the self-assured, instinctive Lone Wolf?

_____

_____

_____

_____

_____

# EXERCISES

## Persona Alignment Exercise :

**1**

*WHAT DO YOU THINK?*

Consider the traits of every sales persona and determine which most closely matches your present strategy. Think about how you may modify your style to include aspects of the Challenger profile.

_____

_____

_____

_____

## Play Role-Playing Exercises :

**2**

*WHAT DO YOU THINK?*

Take part in role-playing games in which you represent several sales personas, especially the Challenger. To improve your flexibility, engage in forceful arguments and have a thorough grasp of the companies of your clients.

_____

_____

_____

## Team Persona Mapping :

**3**

*WHAT DO YOU THINK?*

Work with your sales team to identify the primary sales persona for each member. Talk about the ways in which a varied mix of personalities might enhance the success and general efficacy of the team.

_____

_____

_____

_____

How much do you integrate personal growth and feedback into your sales approach that is consistent with the traits of a Hard Worker?

_____

_____

_____

_____

_____

_____

_____

Which is your preference: establishing rapport with potential customers (Relationship Builder) or having robust conversations with customers (Challenger)?

_____

_____

_____

_____

_____

_____

How does your whole sales strategy fit with your perception of yourself as a problem-solver who is dependable and detail-oriented?

_____

_____

_____

_____

_____

_____

How do you strike a balance in your sales contacts between the necessity to provide results and the difficulties of being a difficult customer (Lone Wolf)?

_____

_____

_____

_____

_____

_____

Are you actively trying to close the performance difference between top performers and core performers, particularly if your strategy fits the Challenger profile?

_____

_____

_____

_____

_____

_____

Given the efficacy of the Challenger method, what actions can you do to improve your abilities and conduct in this manner?

_____

_____

_____

_____

_____

# FINAL RESULTS
# TRACKER

## THE MOST IMPORTANT GOAL I ACHIEVED

## HOW DID I ACHIEVE IT?

## PERSONAL NOTE :

## HOW CAN I KEEP IT UP

## THINGS I'M GRATEFUL FOR:

## LESSONS LEARNED

# CHAPTER 3

## UNCOVERING THE QUALITIES OF A CHALLENGER REPRESENTATIVE

The third chapter of "The Challenger Sale" delves further into the characteristics that set a Challenger sales professional apart. These characteristics, which are distilled into a small number of essential skills, set Challenger representatives apart from their competitors and highlight their critical role in achieving favorable sales results.

Offering a Customer a Distinctive Viewpoint: A representative from Challenger stands out when they provide clients with an alternative viewpoint. They provide perspectives and expertise that beyond the client's present comprehension, enhancing the interaction with new ideas and creative fixes.

b. Having Strong Bidirectional Communication Skills: The capacity to have meaningful and active two-way conversations is essential to the Challenger profile. This entails actively listening to the requirements, worries, and comments of the client in addition to successfully communicating information. The Challenger is excellent at creating a lively and cooperative conversation.

c. Being Aware of the Customer Value Drivers: A Challenger representative goes above and beyond the obvious in their contacts, digging deep to uncover the complex value drivers that compel and sway the consumer. With this knowledge, they may adjust their strategy to better suit the unique requirements and goals of the client.

d. Determining the Economic Forces Behind a Prospect's Enterprise: A Challenger is exceptional at figuring out the economic drivers of a prospect's firm, even beyond knowing consumer value. Because of this astute observation, they are able to match their presentation to the core economic ideas that influence the prospects' choices.

e. Comfortable Conversations About Money: The Challenger is not afraid to bring up money issues in conversation. They seem at ease and self-assured while discussing the money side of the transaction, realizing how important budgetary factors are when making decisions.

f. Being Able to Put the Customer Under Positive Pressure: The Challenger representative's ability to strategically apply pressure is a complex talent. Instead of using force, this strategy involves gently urging the consumer to face their prejudices and inspiring them to think constructively about other viewpoints and methods.

Characteristics of a Challenger Representative:

Three fundamental skills are what "The Challenger Sale" distills into the essence of a Challenger representative:

a. Educating Clients on Unknown Information: Challengers do well in school. They do more for their clients than only offer goods or services; they also educate them on things that they may not know. This teaching position also includes advising on how to successfully navigate and compete in their market.

b. Customizing the Sales Pitch to the Needs of the Decision-Maker: Challenger representatives exhibit flexibility by customizing their sales proposal to meet the demands of decision-makers.

This tailored strategy guarantees that the presentation will be understood by the important decision-makers.

c. Taking Charge of the Talk About Pricing: The price conversation is led by a challenger, who pushes the conversation in a way that contradicts the customer's assumptions. This is asking pointed questions and offering an alternative viewpoint to get the client to reconsider their presumptions and concerns around cost.

The chapter delves into the nuances of these distinguishing characteristics, illuminating how a Challenger representative applies them to effectively handle challenging sales situations. It acts as a manual for salespeople hoping to adopt the Challenger strategy, providing them with insights into the subtle abilities that distinguish them in the ever-changing world of business-to-business sales.

# Key Lessons

## Lesson 1 :  Viewpoint and Understanding

Acknowledge the significance of offering clients a distinct viewpoint and insightful information that goes beyond what they already comprehend.

## Lesson 2 :  Good Communication

Acknowledge the importance of having strong two-way communication abilities, which include both efficiently communicating information and paying attention to what customers need to say.

## Lesson 3 :  Comprehending Value Drivers

Recognize the need of thoroughly examining the factors that drive and impact consumer choices, and adjust your strategy appropriately.

## Lesson 4 :  Interpreting Economic Drivers

Recognize the need of figuring out a prospect's business's economic drivers in order to match sales presentations with core concepts of decision-making.

## Lesson 5 :  Be at Ease with Financial Conversations

Gain assurance and comfort while engaging in financial conversations, and recognize the critical role that budgetary concerns play in the decision-making process.

### Skill Enhancement Blueprint

**NOTE**

Create a thorough strategy to improve your capacity to communicate, to be flexible when creating sales proposals, and to hone your strategic pressure application abilities.

---

### Effort for Educational Contribution

**NOTE**

To demonstrate your function as both a sales person and an educator, start an effort to actively provide educational insights to consumers.

---

### Strategy for Aligning Decision-Makers

**NOTE**

Develop a plan for precisely matching your sales presentations to the needs of decision-makers so that you resonate with the important players who influence the purchase.

| Goals | Action Plan |
| --- | --- |
|  |  |
|  |  |
|  |  |
|  |  |
|  |  |
|  |  |
|  |  |
|  |  |
|  |  |

## Final Results

In your sales encounters, how well do you provide consumers a distinct viewpoint and insightful information?

_____

_____

_____

_____

_____

_____

Do you have strong two-way communication abilities that include both providing information effectively and paying attention to what customers need?

_____

_____

_____

_____

_____

How much do you research the factors that impact client choices and adjust your strategy accordingly?

_____

_____

_____

_____

_____

How effectively can you pinpoint a prospect's company's economic factors such that your sales presentation is in line with basic principles of decision-making?

_____

_____

_____

_____

_____

_____

Do you feel at ease and certain when talking about money concerns, understanding the critical role that budgetary factors play in the decision-making process?

_____

_____

_____

_____

_____

_____

How do you intentionally use pressure to get clients to reevaluate their viewpoints in a positive way?

_____

_____

_____

_____

_____

_____

How much do you steer price
conversations to get customers
to reconsider their
presumptions and question their
way of thinking?

_____

_____

_____

_____

_____

_____

_____

Are you proactively fostering
flexibility in your sales
presentations to accommodate a
range of decision-maker needs?

_____

_____

_____

_____

_____

_____

_____

Do you think you might be more
at ease and confident in financial
talks, knowing how important
they are to the decision-making
process?

_____

_____

_____

_____

_____

_____

# EXERCISES

### Role-playing Games :

**1**

WHAT DO YOU THINK?

Situations that Call for You to Provide Customers with a Different Viewpoint and Useful Insights: Play role-playing games that will help you hone your ability to change viewpoints.

## Communication Skills Audit :

**2**

WHAT DO YOU THINK?

Ask mentors or coworkers for comments on your communication abilities. Point up specific areas where you can do better at both active listening and informational delivery.

## Workshop on Customizing Sales Pitches :

**3**

WHAT DO YOU THINK?

Work with colleagues to create and improve sales pitches that are targeted at certain decision-makers. Exchange ideas and criticism to improve flexibility while handling a range of needs.

In what ways do you now use strategic pressure in your sales strategy, and how can you improve this ability to produce more positive results?

How much of an educator do you consider yourself to be in your sales profession, and how can you further educate your clients?

Are you aware of what decision-makers need and actively adjusting your sales presentations to suit their particular requirements?

# FINAL RESULTS TRACKER

## THE MOST IMPORTANT GOAL I ACHIEVED

## HOW DID I ACHIEVE IT?

## PERSONAL NOTE :

## HOW CAN I KEEP IT UP

## THINGS I'M GRATEFUL FOR:

## LESSONS LEARNED

# Chapter 4

## ADAPTIVE EDUCATION FOR MARKET DISTINCTION

In this Chapter, the author makes a bold claim: the days of solution selling are passing. According to the authors, consumers are not as likely to take the time to help salespeople understand their demands in the modern environment. Rather, they support a paradigm change in favor of transformational education, a strategy that has a greater effect. The chapter elaborates on seven crucial aspects that work together to provide a satisfying client experience.

Distinctive/Valuable Market Viewpoint: A sales representative who provides a distinctive and relevant viewpoint in the market is the first building block of a pleasant client experience. The representative turns the exchange from a transaction into a life-changing experience by offering perspectives that go beyond the norm.

Helping to Discover Substitutions: Clients like a salesperson that does more than just pitch one product. A successful sales contact gives the consumer a thorough understanding of all available options, enabling them to make well-informed selections.

Constant Guidance and Counsel: Good customer service is not limited to the original sale. The significance of a sales representative offering continuing guidance and consultation is emphasized in the third section. Continuous value addition is ensured by this dynamic involvement, even after the sale.

HELPING to Prevent Problems: Effective sales representatives are known for their proactive approach to problem-solving. The representative improves the customer experience by becoming a trusted partner in the client's journey by helping them recognize and prevent possible issues.

Teaching New Problems and Their Consequences: In a company environment that is changing quickly, clients appreciate representatives who are also instructors. In addition to adding value, a representative who proactively educates clients about novel problems and possible solutions establishes oneself as a thought leader.

Purchase Ease: A favorable customer experience is shaped in large part by the simplicity of purchase, even in situations other than sales interactions. The need of making sure the purchase process is efficient and user-friendly is emphasized throughout the chapter.

Broad-Based Organizational Assistance: The last component focuses on organizational assistance. Customers have a more favorable impression of a provider when they see broad support for them inside the company. Throughout the client journey, a flawless experience is guaranteed by this support network.

Realizing that consumers now want more from a connection than just a transaction is the main lesson to be learned from this chapter. They lust for participation that offers value, wisdom, and continuous assistance. These consumer expectations are in line with the transformational teaching style that the authors support, signaling a change toward a more engaging and dynamic sales contact. These seven categories serve as a roadmap for salespeople starting their path of difference and turning good client experiences into enduring ones.

# Key Lessons

## Lesson 1 :  **Change from Solution Selling**

Recognize that solution selling is becoming less successful and adopt a transformational teaching strategy to increase client involvement.

## Lesson 2 :  **Customer Experience Priorities**

Identify the seven essential components that work together to create a satisfying customer experience. These components include distinct viewpoints, help in identifying options, continuous guidance, problem prevention, learning about new topics, simplicity of purchase, and organizational support.

## Lesson 3 :  **Value Beyond Transactions**

Acknowledge that clients want connections that go beyond simple transactions and instead provide them with continuous value, advice, and assistance.

## <u>Transformational Teaching Integration</u>

<u>NOTE</u>

Create a thorough strategy that highlights continuous value, understanding, and assistance in order to include transformational teaching ideas into your sales strategy.

## <u>Initiative for Improved Customer Engagement</u>

<u>NOTE</u>

Assemble your team and take the lead in implementing the seven essential areas into your sales contacts in order to actively improve customer engagement.

## <u>Enhancing Organizational Support</u>

<u>NOTE</u>

Create a plan to improve organizational support in your network of suppliers so that customers have a smooth and encouraging experience all the way through.

| Goals | Action Plan |
| --- | --- |
|  |  |
|  |  |
|  |  |
|  |  |
|  |  |
|  |  |
|  |  |
|  |  |
|  |  |

## Final Results

How well do you conduct sales contacts by offering a distinct and important viewpoint in the market?

_____
_____
_____
_____
_____
_____

How can you help clients look at options instead than pushing only one particular solution?

_____
_____
_____
_____
_____
_____

After your consumers' first purchase, do you actively continue to provide them assistance and consultation?

_____
_____
_____
_____
_____

In what proactive ways do you, as a sales person, help clients recognize and steer clear of such issues?

_____
_____
_____

_____
_____
_____
_____

How much do you go above and beyond to inform clients about fresh problems and possible solutions in the constantly changing business environment?

_____
_____
_____

_____
_____
_____
_____

How simple and easy is it for clients to utilize the purchase procedure that you provide?

_____
_____
_____

_____
_____
_____
_____

How do you make sure that your supplier network has broad organizational support in order to provide a flawless client experience?

_____

_____

_____

_____

_____

_____

Have you seen a change in the expectations of your customers toward more engaging and dynamic sales interactions?

_____

_____

_____

_____

_____

_____

Do you see the significance of participation that goes beyond just transactional interactions and provides value, insight, and continuous support?

_____

_____

_____

_____

_____

# EXERCISES

### Value-Added Sales presentation :

**1**

WHAT DO YOU THINK?

Create a sales presentation that highlights the features that add value to your product or service and includes components that correspond with the seven main points that were covered.

## Customer Journey Map :

**2**

WHAT DO YOU THINK?

Work together with your team to create a customer journey map that shows all the touchpoints where continuing guidance, instruction, and assistance may be easily included.

## Organizational Support Audit :

**3**

WHAT DO YOU THINK?

Evaluate your supplier network's degree of organizational support. Determine areas that need improvement and create plans to increase assistance for a more satisfying experience for customers.

Are you using the transformational teaching methodology that the book advocates in conjunction with your sales approach?

_____

_____

_____

_____

_____

_____

_____

How can you improve your capacity to provide clients continuous guidance and advise throughout their experience using your good or service?

_____

_____

_____

_____

_____

_____

_____

How much do you actively help clients avoid problems by establishing oneself as a reliable companion along the way?

_____

_____

_____

_____

_____

How frequently do you position yourself as a thought leader by educating consumers about new challenges and possible consequences throughout your sales interactions?

_____

_____

_____

_____

_____

_____

What adjustments can you make to simplify and make it easier for your consumers to make purchases?

_____

_____

_____

_____

_____

_____

Is your supplier network actively cultivating broad organizational support in order to ensure a smooth client experience?

_____

_____

_____

_____

_____

_____

# FINAL RESULTS TRACKER

## THE MOST IMPORTANT GOAL  I ACHIEVED

## HOW DID I ACHIEVE IT?

## PERSONAL NOTE :

## HOW CAN I KEEP IT UP

## THINGS I'M GRATEFUL FOR:

## LESSONS LEARNED

# Chapter 5

## UNMATCHED DIFFERENTIATION VIA MASTERY of COMMERCIAL TEACHING

The authors of "The Challenger Sale" introduce a revolutionary method of instruction called "Commercial Teaching" in the book's crucial Chapter 5. With the help of this cutting-edge approach, sales representatives can now educate prospects on how to consider their own needs in addition to selling goods or services —a skill set that distinguishes top-performing reps. This chapter provides sales professionals looking to stand out in a crowded market with a road map of the six key elements that make up a successful commercial teaching presentation.

1. The Heater: The first part of the teaching pitch, "The Warmer," emphasizes the value of demonstrating a thorough comprehension of the prospect's issues. This compassionate start creates a vital link and prepares the audience for the next educational adventure.

2. The Reframe: The second element, "The Reframe," improves the pitch by relating the prospect's difficulties to a larger, more important problem or opportunity that they may not have previously seen. This rephrasing prepares the potential for a radical change in viewpoint.

3. Reasonable Submersion: The third element, "Rational Drowning," deliberately points out to prospects the flaws in their existing way of thinking.

It eloquently demonstrates why altering their strategy is not only advantageous but also necessary to overcome the difficulties they encounter.

4. Impact on Emotions: Part four, "Emotional Impact," adds emotional relevance to the story by exploring the everyday struggles that prospects face in their company. The prospect's connection to the need for change is strengthened by the emotionally driven tale.

5. A Novel Approach: The possibility is presented with a fresh viewpoint in the fifth component. "A New Way" is persuading them of the benefits of your offering and presenting a novel viewpoint that compels them to reevaluate how they plan to handle the current problems.

6. Your Remedy: The pitch culminates in the last section, "Your Solution," which describes how your product or service differs from the competitors. This section presents your solution as the best option by highlighting how well it fits the new perspective on the company.

Essentially, being an expert in Commercial Teaching is a matter of skillfully integrating these six elements into an engaging story that leads potential clients on a path of transformation. Selling isn't the only thing to do; you also need to provide potential customers a fresh perspective on their problems and demonstrate how your solution neatly fits in with this new understanding.

It is recommended that sales professionals who want to stand out from the competition absorb these elements and work on improving their commercial teaching pitch so that it not only fulfills the requirements of prospects but also changes the way they see those demands. By doing this, they open the door to a more meaningful interaction that goes beyond traditional sales techniques.

# Key Lessons

## Lesson 1 : **Mastery of Commercial Teaching**

Acknowledge the need of implementing a Commercial Teaching strategy, which goes beyond conventional sales tactics by enabling representatives to educate potential customers on how to formulate their needs.

## Lesson 2 : **Six Crucial Elements**

As a guide for difference and transformational engagement, internalize the six elements of a strong commercial teaching pitch: The Warmer, The Reframe, Rational Drowning, Emotional Impact, A New Way, and Your Solution.

## Lesson 3 : **Emotional Resonance**

Recognize the critical role that emotions play in storytelling, and use prospects' everyday problems to build a strong connection and emphasize the need for change.

**Action Plan 1**

### <u>Individual Pitch Enhancement strategy</u>

<u>NOTE</u>

Create a customized strategy with clear objectives and doable actions to improve your commercial teaching pitch.

---

**Action Plan 1**

### <u>Team Training Initiative</u>

<u>NOTE</u>

Hold a training session on Commercial Teaching for the whole team, developing a common understanding of the methodology and offering helpful advice on its implementation.

---

**Action Plan 1**

### <u>Common Observations and Ideas</u>

<u>NOTE</u>

Establish a feedback and iteration procedure within your team to promote ongoing improvement of commercial teaching proposals by drawing on common observations and ideas.

| Goals | Action Plan |
|---|---|
| | |
| | |
| | |
| | |
| | |
| | |
| | |
| | |
| | |

## Final Results

In the first part of your sales presentation, how well do you demonstrate that you understand the issues that your prospect is facing?

_____

_____

_____

_____

_____

_____

_____

How can you connect prospects' difficulties to more expansive options that they may not have previously considered?

_____

_____

_____

_____

_____

_____

_____

_____

Are you effectively pointing out to potential customers the flaws in their present way of thinking and getting them to realize that they must change?

_____

_____

_____

_____

_____

How much do you tie your sales story to the everyday struggles that prospects face in your company by adding emotional resonance?

_____

_____

_____

_____

_____

_____

_____

How can you persuade potential customers of the worth of your good or service while offering a novel viewpoint on their problems throughout your pitches?

_____

_____

_____

_____

_____

Are you able to skillfully combine the six elements of a commercial teaching pitch into a coherent and engaging story?

_____

_____

_____

_____

_____

What changes can you make to your Commercial Teaching strategy to better match it with the transformational journey that you want to lead prospects through?

Are you only trying to sell a product, or are you actively educating potential customers about how to consider their needs in a wider context?

After using the Commercial Teaching technique, have you seen a change in the prospect's viewpoint, particularly in terms of seeing the need for change?

# EXERCISES

## Pitch Refinement Workshop :

**1**

*WHAT DO YOU THINK?*

Work together with peers to assess and improve one another's commercial teaching pitches, paying particular attention to how the six components flow naturally together.

## Effect on Emotions Storytelling Session :

**2**

*WHAT DO YOU THINK?*

Hold a storytelling session where team members share narratives that highlight their emotional effect, whether they are personal or professional. Talk about the integration of these stories into sales presentations.

## Prospect Perspective Analysis :

**3**

*WHAT DO YOU THINK?*

Examine previous sales interactions to find situations when the prospect's viewpoint changed noticeably. Analyze how successful the commercial teaching strategy is in these situations.

Are you using emotional impact in your narrative to connect with prospects on a deep level?

_____

_____

_____

_____

_____

_____

_____

How much does your proposal reveal a fresh way of thinking and influence prospects to reevaluate how they tackle challenges?

_____

_____

_____

_____

_____

_____

Are you demonstrating the special worth of your offering and how it fits in with the recently developed business viewpoint?

_____

_____

_____

_____

_____

_____

Have you determined where
your commercial teaching pitch
needs work in order to have a
more revolutionary effect?

_____
_____
_____
_____
_____
_____

Are you providing prospects
with a fresh perspective on their
problems in your sales
interactions that goes beyond
traditional sales techniques?

_____
_____
_____
_____
_____
_____

Are you aware of how leading
prospects on a trip that alters
their understanding of their own
needs may have a transforming
effect?

_____
_____
_____
_____
_____

# FINAL RESULTS
# TRACKER

## THE MOST IMPORTANT GOAL  I ACHIEVED

## HOW DID I ACHIEVE IT?

## PERSONAL NOTE :

## HOW CAN I KEEP IT UP

## THINGS I'M GRATEFUL FOR:

## LESSONS LEARNED

# Chapter 6

## CREATING PERSONALIZED IMPACT IN SALES

In this chapter six, a novel approach is presented: customizing sales tactics to create resonance. The chapter explores important elements that reinterpret the sales flow, highlighting the skill of fostering agreement among stakeholders. The following are the main ideas and revelations in this revolutionary chapter:

1. Constructing Consensus: AN ART, Finding agreement throughout the business is the biggest obstacle decision-makers confront, according to research. The challenger model acknowledges the need to go above and beyond by educating end users about the nuances of their companies, while the traditional strategy concentrates on stakeholders in order to clinch a deal. The way to enduring harmony in a contract is to have a thorough understanding throughout the whole firm.

2. The New Channel of Sales: The challenger model places more emphasis on a strong relationship between the salesperson and the stakeholder than the standard sales model, which involves representatives gathering information from stakeholders to convey to higher authorities. The new sales flow emphasizes using this relationship to complete business and acknowledges the critical role stakeholders play in influencing decision-makers.

3. Customizing for Involved Parties: The challenger model promotes a greater emphasis on interacting with stakeholders, first at the level of the industry and then going into the finer points of the company and individual positions.

Tailored messaging based on client results is the key to successful customization. In order to ensure a more comprehensive grasp of client demands, this strategy requires representatives to contact a wider range of stakeholders than before.

In "The Challenger Sale," Solae Story:

One interesting example is the story of Solae, a company that makes soy-based food components. In response to the difficulty of an increasing number of stakeholders, Solae launched Customer Outcomes Cards in a creative way. These cards gave representatives a thorough tool to comprehend important stakeholders and their intended results by summarizing their issues and goals.

Solae's sales approach makes use of the client Outcomes Cards as a framework for documenting client buy-in. Stakeholders are requested to sign off on the template, and the recorded agreement is shown as proof of alignment across the whole company at the last meeting with the decision-maker. Because every stakeholder is seen as a consumer in Solae's unique approach, consensus building is even more important.

The main takeaway from this chapter is the realization that teaching end customers and creating consensus inside the company are equally important components of resonant sales, in addition to engaging stakeholders. It promotes a flexible strategy that adjusts messaging to each stakeholder according to their intended results, which eventually results in a more thorough and successful sales plan.

# Key Lessons

## Lesson 1 : **Priority Consensus Building**

Acknowledge that reaching agreement inside the organization is the biggest obstacle for decision-makers. Adapt your sales strategy to go beyond stakeholders and educate end users in order to promote thorough comprehension and long-lasting peace in transactions.

## Lesson 2 : **Suppliers' Strategic Positioning**

The challenger model, which emphasizes a strong connection between sales representatives and stakeholders, replaces the traditional sales model that emphasized the relationship between representatives and decision-makers. This results in new sales flow dynamics. Make the most of this relationship to successfully influence decision-makers and complete transactions.

## Lesson 3 : **Stakeholder-Centric Tailoring**

Adopt a stakeholder-centric strategy by interacting with a wider range of stakeholders, beginning with the industry and working your way down to the intricacies of individual jobs and organizations. Tailor communications to the needs of your audience in order to maximize impact and effectiveness.

## Lesson 4 : **Solae's Creative Approach**

Take a cue from Solae's creative approach, which makes use of Customer Outcomes Cards to comprehend and attend to the needs of all parties involved. Utilize templates and other tools to document consumer support and show agreement when having last-minute conversations with decision-makers.

## Action Plan 1

### Tailoring Enhancement strategy

**NOTE**

Create a customized strategy that integrates input from simulations, real-world situations, and stakeholder mapping to improve your tailoring approach.

## Action Plan 1

### Consensus-Building project

**NOTE**

Set out to emphasize consensus-building inside the company by launching a team-wide project. Establish clear procedures, roles, and duties to promote a more cooperative sales atmosphere.

## Action Plan 1

### Innovation in Sales Strategy

**NOTE**

Form a task group tasked with investigating novel approaches in sales, using cues from Solae's methodology and other sector instances. Apply the knowledge you've gained to modify and improve your sales approach for impact and efficiency.

| Goals | Action Plan |
|-------|-------------|
|       |             |
|       |             |
|       |             |
|       |             |
|       |             |
|       |             |
|       |             |
|       |             |

## Final Results

To what extent does your sales strategy emphasize consensus building inside the company as a critical component?

_____
_____
_____
_____
_____
_____
_____

How may your sales strategy be adjusted to go beyond stakeholders and actively include and educate end users about the nuances of their businesses?

_____
_____
_____
_____
_____

Have you seen a change in the way your sales flow operates, from a purely decision-maker-focused approach to one that acknowledges the significance and impact of stakeholders?

_____
_____
_____
_____

How much are you using the
solid relationship that exists ————————————————
between sales representatives
and stakeholders to sway ————————————————
judgment and increase contract ————————————————
closing rates?

————————————————

————————————————

————————————————

How can you ensure resonance
and success in your sales ————————————————
contacts by personalizing ————————————————
messaging according to certain
consumer results to improve ————————————————
your tailoring approach?
————————————————

————————————————

————————————————

Are you actively attempting to ————————————————
comprehend the issues and goals
that each stakeholder has, using ————————————————
instruments like Customer ————————————————
Outcomes Cards to have a more
thorough understanding? ————————————————

————————————————

————————————————

————————————————

Have you thought about recording consumer support and showcasing consensus utilizing templates as a strong argument in last-minute meetings with decision-makers?

How can you connect with Solae's aim to develop a more inclusive and consensus-driven sales approach by treating every stakeholder like a customer?

Do you see how treating stakeholders like clients may promote a more comprehensive understanding and alignment inside the company?

# EXERCISES

## Workshop on Stakeholder Mapping :

**1**

*WHAT DO YOU THINK?*

Assemble your team, identify important stakeholders at different levels, and come up with customized messaging for each group.

_____

_____

_____

_____

## Role-playing Exercise :

**2**

*WHAT DO YOU THINK?*

Conduct a role-playing exercise where team members practice customizing messages according to individual, organizational, and industry-level factors. Exchange ideas and criticism to make improvements.

_____

_____

_____

_____

## Case Study on Consensus-Building :

**3**

*WHAT DO YOU THINK?*

Examine a case study or actual situation where agreement-building was essential to closing a transaction. Talk about the tactics used and draw conclusions that apply to your sales strategy.

_____

_____

_____

_____

How has your sales strategy
changed to include end users in
the education process, realizing
their importance in bringing
about long-term harmony and
agreement in transactions?

How much are you actively
trying to build a relationship
between sales representatives
and stakeholders, realizing how
important it is to influence
decision-makers?

Have you looked at cutting-edge
methods to better comprehend
and handle the problems of each
stakeholder, such as Solae's
Customer Outcomes Cards?

During crucial conversations with decision-makers, are you successfully documenting customer buy-in and offering concrete evidence of agreement utilizing templates and tools?

How can you improve resonance and effectiveness by coordinating your sales plan with the dynamic approach that the challenger model advocates?

Recognizing the importance of a better relationship between sales representatives and stakeholders on total deal closing rates, how can you modify your sales flow to highlight this?

# FINAL RESULTS TRACKER

## THE MOST IMPORTANT GOAL I ACHIEVED

## HOW DID I ACHIEVE IT?

### PERSONAL NOTE:

## HOW CAN I KEEP IT UP

## THINGS I'M GRATEFUL FOR:

## LESSONS LEARNED

# CHAPTER 7

## SUCCESSFULLY MANAGING SALES CONTROL

In 'The Challenger Sale,' Chapter 7, the focus is on taking charge of the sales process—an important component that keeps things moving ahead and fosters a friendly conversation about money. The main ideas and tactics discussed in this chapter are as follows:

1. Sales Control Has Two Results: When you take charge of the transaction, two important things happen:

- a. Leading the Sales Process: The capacity to maintain the sales process's forward motion while providing direction and purpose.
- b. Ensuring Financial Comfort: Expertly handling financial conversations, particularly when they include discounts.

2. Declining Discounts with Confidence: Challengers are self-assured enough to refuse discounts since they think they have added value by teaching clients about things they were unaware of. They seize the initiative by teaching clients about the complexities of procuring intricate solutions and motivating them to approach problems from novel angles.

3. The Balanced Approach to Pushback: Challengers take a measured stance when responding to consumer demands for reductions. They respond with information and analysis, reiterating their position without using force. Good sales control is characterized by the Challenger's ability to lead the client without being unduly aggressive.

4. Eliminating the Fear of Aggression: "The Challenger Sale" debunks the unjustified notion that being forceful breeds hostility. Salespeople often worry that being too forceful might turn off clients. This anxiety is a result of the belief that consumers are in charge, which makes salespeople act passively.

The book emphasizes how crucial it is to acknowledge and share the value and knowledge the organization offers.

DuPont's Method of Control:

DuPont is a prime example of a business that lets its representatives take charge, particularly while negotiating. DuPont evaluates its power position in relation to a number of factors, including brand, price, and product strengths and weaknesses, using a framework for pre-negotiation preparation. Representatives are better able to handle negotiations with confidence when they have a clear idea of the value they offer to the negotiation thanks to this careful preparation.

The Four-Step DuPont Negotiation Framework:

Recognize and Defer: DuPont representatives concede to work on a discount when pressed by customers, but they ask for more time to fully comprehend the client's requirements. They are able to build creative tension and contribute value in this way, giving themselves more time for deliberate bargaining

- Expand and Deepen: Sales representatives explore client demands and pinpoint solutions that fulfill them. The goal of this phase is to let the client understand the actual worth of the suggested solution.
- Investigate and Contrast: DuPont examines possibilities that preserve margins while providing value to the client by analyzing different trade-offs.
- Adhere to the Plan: It's important to decide what, when, and how to give in. DuPont stresses that in order to effectively navigate discussions, compromises must be properly planned.

DuPont's method basically shows how controlling the negotiating process requires careful preparation, comprehension of value arguments, and tactical concession management.

# Key Lessons

## Lesson 1 : **Trust in Value Creation**

Acknowledge that the confidence you have in creating value by enlightening clients about elements they were unaware of before is the foundation for taking charge.

## Lesson 2 : **Balanced Pushback**

Take a measured attitude when responding, relying on facts and insights to support your position without resorting to needless hostility.

## Lesson 3 : **Eliminating the Fear**

Get over your apprehension about coming out as too pushy by acknowledging and articulating the value and knowledge your business offers.

## Lesson 4 : **Strategic Negotiation**

Adopt a strategy that follows DuPont's four-step framework, recognizing, probing, examining, and yielding in accordance with a well-planned strategy.

**Action Plan 1**

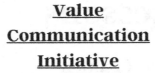

### <u>Value Communication Initiative</u>

<u>NOTE</u>

Create a thorough program to improve team communication on the benefits and knowledge your business offers. Incorporate both practical tasks and training sessions.

**Action Plan 1**

### <u>Negotiation Mastery Program</u>

<u>NOTE</u>

Using DuPont's four-step framework as a model, implement a negotiation mastery program within your team. Give representatives the tools, instruction, and continuous assistance they need to succeed in negotiations.

**Action Plan 1**

### <u>Fear-Disppelling Campaign</u>

<u>NOTE</u>

Initiate a team-wide initiative aimed at eliminating unfounded anxieties around assertiveness. Encourage a culture that aggressively tackles concerns about aggressiveness and supports forceful yet customer-centric methods.

| Goals | Action Plan |
| --- | --- |
|  |  |
|  |  |
|  |  |
|  |  |
|  |  |
|  |  |
|  |  |
|  |  |
|  |  |

## Final Results

How comfortable are you declining discounts knowing that your customer education has added value?

_____
_____
_____

_____
_____
_____
_____

How do you strike a balance in your sales contacts between being forceful and taking a customer-centric approach?

_____
_____
_____

_____
_____
_____
_____

Have you taken proactive steps to allay team members' concerns about assertiveness turning into aggression?

_____
_____

_____
_____
_____
_____

What actions can you do to guarantee that your representatives understand and successfully convey the worth and competence of your business?

_____

_____

_____

_____

_____

_____

How can you provide your team the freedom to lead negotiations by using a similar strategic approach to DuPont's?

_____

_____

_____

_____

_____

_____

How much do you emphasize moving the sales process along while making sure every encounter has a goal and a direction?

_____

_____

_____

_____

_____

What circumstances have you been able to refuse a customer's request without going too far?

_____

_____

_____

_____

_____

_____

Have you evaluated how fear affects the assertiveness of your staff and how it could affect how customers see them?

_____

_____

_____

_____

_____

_____

What strategies can you use to help your team feel more confident about the contributions they make to negotiations?

_____

_____

_____

_____

_____

_____

# EXERCISES

### Workshop on Assertiveness :

**1**

WHAT DO YOU THINK?

Hold a session on assertiveness training, going over situations when being assertive is both useful and required in a sales setting.

## Role-playing Activities :

**2**

WHAT DO YOU THINK?

Participate in role-playing activities that simulate negotiating situations with your team. Stress the need of strategic planning, measured pushback, and skillful concession handling.

## Negotiation Simulation:

**3**

WHAT DO YOU THINK?

A negotiation simulation that is influenced by DuPont's pre-negotiation planning template may be created. Representatives should be encouraged to use the template and assess how it affects their approaches to negotiation.

Is there any particular aspect of
your sales process where gaining
greater authority might improve
overall performance?

_____

_____

_____

_____

_____

_____

_____

How can a well-balanced
pushback strategy be put into
practice that guides consumers
without alienating them by
using data and insights?

_____

_____

_____

_____

_____

_____

How do you now deal with
salespeople' unfounded anxieties,
especially those concerning
assertiveness and customer-
centric approaches?

_____

_____

_____

_____

_____

_____

Which facets of your business's worth and competence need improved team and customer communication?

_____

_____

_____

_____

_____

_____

_____

To empower your representatives during negotiations, have you thought about using pre-negotiation planning tools like DuPont's template?

_____

_____

_____

_____

_____

_____

What actions can you take to guarantee that your representatives have the self-assurance necessary to handle requests for discounts from customers?

_____

_____

_____

_____

_____

# FINAL RESULTS TRACKER

## THE MOST IMPORTANT GOAL I ACHIEVED

## HOW DID I ACHIEVE IT?

## PERSONAL NOTE :

## HOW CAN I KEEP IT UP

## THINGS I'M GRATEFUL FOR:

## LESSONS LEARNED

# CHAPTER 8

## ENHANCING SALES ADMINISTRATION TO ENSURE CHALLENGER ACHIEVEMENT

In 'The Challenger Sale,' Chapter 8, the emphasis switches to the critical function that sales managers play in putting the Challenger model for sales into practice. Surprisingly, 63% of CEB members said their managers don't have the abilities needed to advance the sales approach, despite its efficacy. The selling abilities, coaching, and sales innovation are the three high-level components that the chapter highlights as being essential to management success.

1. Mentoring Excellence: Within the Challenger model, three aspects are indicative of effective coaching:

- a. Ongoing Nature: Coaching is a continuous process that changes as each sales representative develops rather than being a one-time thing.
- b. Customized for Each Representative: Coaching is tailored to each representative, taking into account their particular areas of strength and growth.
- c. Emphasis on Behavior, Not Just Knowledge: The Challenger method is reflected in the development and enhancement of behaviors rather than just knowledge.

2. The Sales Coaching Pause Framework: In order to develop coaching proficiency in sales contacts, the book presents the PAUSE framework:

- be Ready for the Coaching Conversation: Encouraging representatives to be ready ahead of time creates consistency throughout coaching meetings.
- Affirm the Relationship: Place a strong emphasis on personal growth and put performance management conversations on hold to create a supportive coaching atmosphere.
- Recognize Expected Behavior: Supervisors get guidance on what to watch out for and observe, which improves their capacity to conduct coaching talks successfully.
- Clearly define behavior change by giving managers guidelines and expectations for giving constructive criticism.
- Instill New Behaviors: To guarantee long-term effects and ongoing development, institutionalize coaching techniques.

3. Promoting Innovation in Sales: Three essential tasks are involved in sales innovation under the Challenger model:

- Research: Working with representatives to find roadblocks that keep negotiations from moving forward.
- Creation: Charting supplier capacities to handle client issues and generate prospects for upselling.
- Sharing: By openly sharing their creative endeavors, successful managers enable representatives to duplicate successful tactics.

While coaching improves familiar habits, innovation gives teams the tools they need to deal with unanticipated circumstances.

In order to help sales representatives develop a challenger attitude, a sales manager should push them to confront consumers in novel ways. Giving representatives industry-specific knowledge helps them customize their proposals. To further facilitate customisation, goal-outlines for certain professions in particular sectors may be created as cheat sheets. Additionally, supervisors are essential in helping representatives learn how to succeed as challengers by imparting knowledge from other salespeople in comparable circumstances.

# Key Lessons

## Lesson 1 : Challenger Model

The Challenger model for sales success is implemented and maintained by sales managers, who are essential to its success.

## Lesson 2 : Coaching Dimensions

A continuous, individualized strategy that focuses on behavior modification is what makes coaching effective in the Challenger model.

## Lesson 3 : Successful Sales Coaching.

The PAUSE framework, which stands for Prepare, Affirm, Understand, Specify, and Embed, offers a methodical approach to successful sales coaching.

## Lesson 4 : Sales Innovation

By looking into obstacles, coming up with fixes, and sharing effective tactics with their teams, sales managers may foster innovation in the sales process.

## Lesson 5 : Promoting a Challenger Attitude

Managers may help representatives develop a Challenger attitude by giving them industry-specific knowledge and pushing them to confront clients in novel ways.

### Coaching Enhancement Program

**NOTE**

Create and put into action a program that emphasizes continuous, individualized coaching with a behavior-focused approach, including the PAUSE framework.

### Initiative for Innovation Integration

**NOTE**

Take the lead in introducing innovative practices into the sales process. Encourage team members to do research, come up with ideas, and share effective tactics.

### Information Exchange Building Culture

**NOTE**

Encourage the team to share expertise by putting in place frequent forums, training sessions, and cooperative activities that promote the exchange of ideas and effective tactics.

| Goals | Action Plan |
|---|---|
|  |  |
|  |  |
|  |  |
|  |  |
|  |  |
|  |  |
|  |  |
|  |  |
|  |  |
|  |  |

## Final Results

To what extent do you think your management style incorporates behavior-focused, targeted, and continuous coaching?

_____

_____

_____

_____

_____

_____

_____

How can you make your coaching interactions more productive by using the PAUSE framework?

_____

_____

_____

_____

_____

_____

_____

Have you deliberately fostered an atmosphere in coaching sessions where talking about performance management is combined with an emphasis on personal development?

_____

_____

_____

_____

_____

How can you improve your comprehension of anticipated actions so that you can provide more focused and helpful coaching feedback?

_____
_____
_____
_____
_____
_____
_____

Where can you more successfully integrate new habits to guarantee long-term effects and ongoing coaching practice improvement?

_____
_____
_____
_____
_____
_____
_____

How have you actively encouraged sales creativity among your colleagues, especially when it comes to identifying obstacles and coming up with answers for problems faced by customers?

_____
_____
_____
_____

What strategies do you use to motivate sales representatives to confront clients in novel ways, cultivating a challenger mentality within the group?

How can you encourage a culture of information sharing and strategy replication among your team by sharing your inventive successes with them?

How well do you recognize each sales representative's individual strengths and areas for growth and adjust your coaching tactics accordingly?

# EXERCISES

## PAUSE framework :

**1**

WHAT DO YOU THINK?

Conduct an interactive session on the PAUSE framework, emphasizing the use of role-playing situations and interactive discussions to strengthen its implementation.

_____

_____

_____

_____

## Innovation Brainstorming Session :

**2**

WHAT DO YOU THINK?

Hold an innovation brainstorming session with your team to discover possible roadblocks in current transactions and jointly develop creative ideas to get beyond them.

_____

_____

_____

_____

## Challenger Mindset Training :

**3**

WHAT DO YOU THINK?

Put in place a program that teaches representatives to think like challengers, includes industry-specific information, and promotes creative ways to close deals.

_____

_____

_____

_____

What actions can you take to ensure that each representative receives ongoing coaching and growth within your team?

_____

_____

_____

_____

_____

_____

In what ways can you improve the way you presently prepare for coaching discussions to ensure consistency and efficacy?

_____

_____

_____

_____

_____

_____

Where else can you prioritize your sales representatives' personal growth more, delegating performance conversations to more productive coaching sessions?

_____

_____

_____

_____

Which creative endeavors have you individually shared with your team, and how have they influenced the group's success as a whole?

_____

_____

_____

_____

_____

_____

Does your team encounter any particular obstacles while working on deals? If so, how can you work with representatives to better understand and resolve these issues?

_____

_____

_____

_____

_____

What actions may you take to develop solutions that connect supplier capabilities to address customer issues and provide chances for upselling?

_____

_____

_____

_____

_____

# FINAL RESULTS TRACKER

## THE MOST IMPORTANT GOAL I ACHIEVED

## HOW DID I ACHIEVE IT?

## PERSONAL NOTE :

## HOW CAN I KEEP IT UP

## THINGS I'M GRATEFUL FOR:

## LESSONS LEARNED

# CHAPTER 9

## HANDLING THE CHALLENGER MODEL'S IMPLEMENTATION

In 'The Challenger Sale,' Chapter 9, the emphasis switches to the practical side of using the Challenger model, providing senior management, marketing leaders, and sales leaders with important takeaways.

1. Sales Leaders' Perspectives:

- a. Recognizing Challengers: The chapter emphasizes how critical it is to discern between genuine Challengers and high-performers. Sales managers need to watch carefully what their teams do in order to spot Challengers.
- b. Handling Lone Wolves: It's advisable to use caution to prevent lone wolves from taking over the company. Even while they may succeed on their own, their methodology might not fit the Challenger model's emphasis on collaboration and insight-driven work.
- c. Finding a Balance Between Training and Recruiting: Although educating current representatives on the Challenger model is important, finding people who naturally possess Challenger qualities is just as important.
- d. Holistic Development: Sales executives should concentrate on the concurrent development of both individual talents and organizational capabilities in order to optimize the advantages of the Challenger model.
- e. Readying for Receptivity: Training salespeople alone is not enough. Prioritize building receptivity inside the company before conducting training, and follow a methodical process when putting the training into action.

2. **Best Practices for Marketing Executives:** Marketing executives should adopt an insight-centric strategy in order to achieve real customer-centricity. It's crucial to provide original ideas that make clients reconsider their course of action.

- a. Unique Value Proposition: The Challenger model cannot be successfully implemented until the supplier's unique value proposition is recognized and communicated. This fundamental component cannot be compromised.
- b. Differentiating Your Company from the Competition: It's important to develop a compelling story that tackles and resolves client complaints in order to set your company apart in a crowded industry.

3. **Senior Management's Strategic Insights:**

- a. Partial Adoption for Behavioral Shift: An organizational behavior shift of note might result from an 80 percent adoption rate of the Challenger model. While a significant transformation should be the first priority, senior management should not insist on full acceptance.
- b. Acknowledging Resistance: It's reasonable to assume that 20 to 30 percent of sales representatives will oppose the transition to the Challenger model. Instead of imposing uniformity, concentrate on maximizing performance across a range of strategies.
- c. Using Terminology: Positively influencing the organizational attitude may be achieved by using terminology's power. The intended behavioral standards may be reinforced by using appropriate vocabulary from the Challenger model.
- d. Customization for Norms: Integration and acceptability of the Challenger model may be facilitated by adjusting its implementation to conform to the norms of conduct that have been developed within the company.

# Key Lessons

## Lesson 1 : Precise Challenger Identification

Sales executives need to be adept at spotting genuine Challengers in their groups, understanding that exceptional work does not always translate into Challenger conduct.

## Lesson 2 : Be Wary of Lone Wolves

Although they could provide unique outcomes, lone wolves' dominance inside the company might not be compatible with the Challenger model's emphasis on collaboration.

## Lesson 3 : Deliberate Recruitment

The key to a successful model implementation is striking a balance between training initiatives and the deliberate recruitment of people who exhibit Challenger characteristics.

## Lesson 4 : Holistic Development

Leaders should concentrate on enhancing both individual competencies and general organizational capacities in order to maximize the advantages of the Challenger model.

## Lesson 5 : Pre-Training Receptivity

Recognize how crucial it is to close the performance gap between top and core performers in order to maintain the sales team's overall efficacy.

## Action Plan 1

### Challenger Recruitment Strategy

**NOTE**

Create and put into action a recruiting strategy that focuses on finding and selecting candidates that possess innate Challenger qualities.

## Action Plan 1

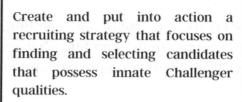

### Initiative for story Integration

**NOTE**

Initiate a project to include the difficult story into customer encounters, communication tactics, and marketing collateral.

## Action Plan 1

### Adoption Optimization Program

**NOTE**

Put in place a program that prioritizes performance enhancement and behavioral changes in order to maximize the effects of the Challenger model's partial adoption (80%).

| Goals | Action Plan |
| --- | --- |
| | |
| | |
| | |
| | |
| | |
| | |
| | |
| | |
| | |

## Final Results

To what extent is your sales force able to discriminate between real Challengers and high achievers?

_____

_____

_____

_____

_____

_____

How do you deal with lone wolves to make sure their strategy fits the cooperative spirit of the Challenger model?

_____

_____

_____

_____

_____

_____

What actions can you take to improve the Challenger model's execution by striking a balance between targeted recruiting and training efforts?

_____

_____

_____

_____

_____

_____

Where in your team can you concentrate on the overall growth of members' capacities as individuals and as an organization?

_____

_____

_____

_____

_____

_____

_____

How may organizational receptivity be established prior to beginning Challenger model sales training?

_____

_____

_____

_____

_____

_____

_____

How can you help your marketing team adopt an insight-centric mindset in order to promote customer-centricity?

_____

_____

_____

_____

_____

_____

_____

How distinct is your company's value offer, and how may it be made more compelling for the Challenger model to succeed?

_____

_____

_____

_____

_____

_____

What techniques can you use to create a difficult story that successfully tackles the problems faced by your target audience?

_____

_____

_____

_____

_____

_____

What is the potential effect of 80 percent adoption of the Challenger model on organizational behavior change in your context?

_____

_____

_____

_____

# EXERCISES

## Workshop on Challenger Model Identification :

**1**

WHAT DO YOU THINK?

Organize a workshop to teach executives how to correctly identify and differentiate Challengers in the sales force.

_____

_____

_____

_____

## Storytelling Workshop :

**2**

WHAT DO YOU THINK?

Lead a group discussion with marketing departments to develop a compelling story that tackles consumer issues and distinguishes the company.

_____

_____

_____

## Adoption Impact Simulation :

**3**

WHAT DO YOU THINK?

Using scenario-based activities and dialogues, simulate the effects of attaining 80% adoption of the Challenger model.

_____

_____

_____

_____

How are you going to handle objections from sales representatives who may not be quick to adopt the Challenger model?

_____

_____

_____

_____

_____

_____

_____

Which terms from the Challenger model may you strategically use to change the organizational mindset?

_____

_____

_____

_____

_____

_____

How might the Challenger model be implemented differently to conform to the behavioral standards already in place in your organization?

_____

_____

_____

_____

_____

Have you recorded your concessions and negotiating sequences in order to develop a more methodical and planned approach?

_____

_____

_____

_____

_____

_____

How can you improve the capacity of your team to strategically examine and contrast trade-offs during negotiations?

_____

_____

_____

_____

_____

In what particular situations have you effectively recognized and postponed requests from customers while adding value to the process?

_____

_____

_____

_____

_____

# FINAL RESULTS TRACKER

## THE MOST IMPORTANT GOAL  I ACHIEVED

## HOW DID I ACHIEVE IT?

## PERSONAL NOTE :

## HOW CAN I KEEP IT UP

## THINGS I'M GRATEFUL FOR:

## LESSONS LEARNED

Made in United States
Orlando, FL
15 December 2024

55754482R00065